The 33 Worst Mistakes Writers Make About Horses

The Secrets Only Insiders Know

WRITE IT RIGHT #1

Becky Burkheart

Previously published as Sue L. Huffman

An A Conspiracy of Authors (ACOA) Publication
www.aconspiracyofauthors.com

ISBN: 978-1-936507-42-9

Text and Cover design: Holly Lisle

Cover Art: Photo image Copyright Becky Burkheart

Photo credits: Becky Huffman, Dan Stanfield, Jacob Huffman, Cindy Stafford, John Adame, Bobbi Sanders of Lone Oak Photography, Carol Sanders, Major Photography - Austin Texas, Leslie Stauffer

First printing 2008

Second Printing, 2011

Third Printing, 2013

About the Author

Becky's first pony came along early in her childhood and by her late teens she was teaching and training professionally. Since discovering AERC endurance riding in the late 80s, running wild through the woods has remained her true love while she's flirted with everything from 4-H, dressage and barrel racing to more esoteric sports such as jousting, mounted archery and Cowboy Mounted Shooting - all on horses she's bred and raised.

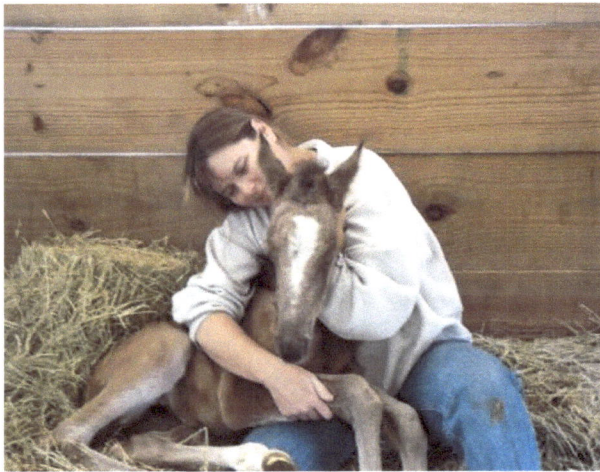

She has a unique perspective into the relationship with a horse, not just from the many horses she's handled over the years, but from the untold hours of riding cross-country, day and night, in varied terrain and under all kinds of conditions.

* Her email: BLUESue22@gmail.com
* Her websites: www.BeckyBurkheart.com and http://bluesue1.blogspot.com/

Table of Contents

Dedication

To my SHADOWFAX,
He taught me to listen to what horses had to say.

Acknowledments

Many Thanks to Leah Breamal http://leahbraemel.blogspot.com/
Tamara Woodcock http://www.aelfleahfarm.com/
Val J http://endurovet.blogspot.com/
Anne McGoy http://www.briarwoodarabian.com/
Sheila Harmon at http://www.destinyarabians.com/
Theresa Chappell, DVM, Kitty Myers, Sue Stewart, Pamela Klein, Christine
Warren, Robin and Robin with RWA Elements, and special thanks to all the ladies
in the Garden.

Introduction

A roomful of horsemen will disagree in five ways on three subjects, and for the most part, it's not a matter of right or wrong, but of personal experience and perspective. And that makes it difficult for authors to know which experience applies to which situation.

What makes my perspective worthwhile? I've been involved with horses a long time, since the '70s and most of what I've learned has come from the school of hard knocks. If there's a mistake to be made, chances are, I've made it.

I'm competitive, but also in it for the fun, and that makes me prone to dabble. I've done ring classes in all kinds of shows, some dressage, lots of fun cowboy stuff like rodeo and speed events and a little cow work. Even medieval and western reenactment - I've used the lance, axe, bow and gun from horseback.

My long time abiding love is the trail and I've been riding AERC Endurance since 1986. So I know about being on horseback all day, galloping in a crowd and being alone in the woods with a horse. I've ridden for miles and hours under the worst kind of conditions and I've ridden when I was so sick I couldn't stand up if I wasn't sitting in the saddle.

I've trained professionally and been a riding instructor, as well as having bred my own horses since the early '90s, so all this fun has been had on a variety of horses, both good and bad.

In writing this book, I'm offering to let you apply my screw-ups, experiences and expertise to your writing. Because I've lived the range from success to the worst wrecks, because I've seen the usual suspects make the same wrong assumptions and errors over and again - both in riding and writing - this book will help you avoid the writing mistakes and show you ways to use the riding mistakes to strengthen and deepen your equine characters and interactions.

I'll answer the questions you didn't know you needed to ask.

The Mistakes

Horses are living, breathing, thinking creatures with strong individualities. They have rigid social structures within the herds and will, on some level, transfer that to the people and other creatures in their world. They're emotional animals with a strong flight instinct that conflicts in many cases with a strong protective instinct.

Throughout our real history, there have been cultures and individuals who celebrated the horse and others who didn't. Fictional horses and horsemen, however fantastical or realistic, should fall within those guidelines. Yet many authors tend to use them only as a type of velveteen window dressing or a passionless means of transportation.

Not just getting the basic facts and terms correct, but giving your horses a little personality can add layers, depth and realism to your world and will help it stay in the readers mind.

Mistake One – Stallions

It seems standard fare to mount the hero on a stallion, but this is a point where authors need careful attention to their cultural nuances and worldbuilding. Most modern heroes aren't going to be riding stallions unless they're equine professionals or male chauvinist assholes with self-esteem issues. European, Middle-eastern and South American cultures are less prone to geld their stallions and Medieval or Fantasy worlds may legitimately mount their heroes on intact males. But many authors use the designation without understanding what a tremendous source of conflict having to manage a 1000lbs or more of testosterone gives their hero.

Riding a stallion is like driving a high performance sports car that has ADHD. I have a stallion; he's the light of my life. He's optimistic and energetic and ambitious. He's personable and sexy beyond all reason. But he demands 120% of my attention at all times. If I needed to cross the mountains to get medicine to the children, I would take him because between me and the mountain, we could keep him focused. If I'm going to an event we've trained for - he does well for me, but he's not a lazy Sunday kind of horse. If you haven't seen Shrek II, watch it. Eddie Murphy plays a fantastic stallion with all his attitude and prancing and posing. I laughed so hard I couldn't breathe. He was perfect.

* I think the main issue authors need to understand is that stallions are all about sex. Certainly they can be trained to behave and not talk trash or posture and strut for the mares, but they are still thinking about it. Every minute. It's simply how they are and it's what they do.

* You'll seldom see a stallion standing quietly and napping unless he's tucked in at home, and then he'll be masturbating - eyes half-closed in a sweet dreamy way as he thumps his erection on his belly. They can't be tied on the hitching post in front of the saloon and they can't be put in a box stall next to a mare or another stallion. They tend to be very destructive. They squeal; they rear and strike and kick; they blow and sniff and snort. They'll flirt with any horse within range, or any scent on the air, or with any person standing nearby. They love the smell of mare poo. If they aren't acting on these urges, they're thinking about them. You'll see it in the bow of their neck, the perk of their ears and the twinkle in their eyes. If they aren't allowed that, they're likely to turn sullen.

Mistake Two - Colors

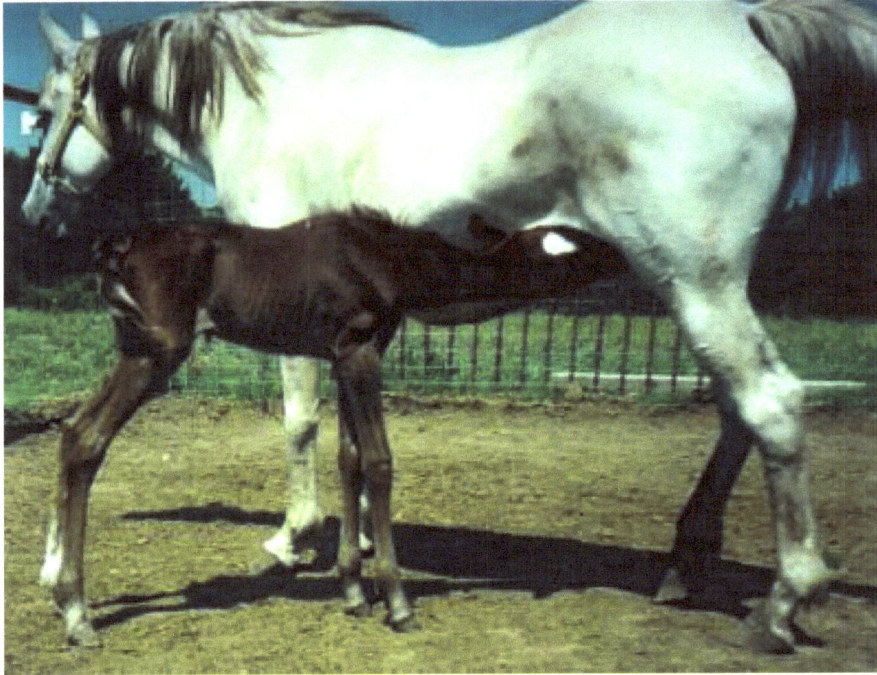

Horse colors are not difficult but this is an area where it pays to spend a few minutes at the library or online looking at "equine color genetics" or "horse colors and markings". One of the main points authors tend to miss is the difference between white horses (pink skin) and grey horses (black skin). White horses are rare because of lethal genetic issues, but they are born white and stay white throughout their lives. And don't forget that pink skin sunburns. A grey horse is born its base color, but "goes grey" as it ages. The author must be aware of the dramatic coat color changes a grey horse goes through over the years, from its base color to rose to steel or silver dapple and eventually fleabitten or to pure white. Grey horses are prone to melanomas at the rate of about 80%, so most older grey horses are going to be lumpy. If you want a common horse to blend into your hero's background, use a chestnut, they blend in well if they are non-descript. If you want a fancy horse that will be noticed, choose an unusual color coat, pattern or markings.

I'll never forget when I picked up a kitten, petted its fluffy-soft fur, looked at the color of its skin, checked the fur for different shadings of color, looked in its little eyes and checked between its toes. I wondered what color it would be when it was grown. My mom looked at me with a blank expression as if I was insane, and my sister almost bust a gut laughing. I didn't know cats are born the color they're going to be because horses aren't. The foal coat is almost always dramatically different from the adult coat. Black horses are mousy colored at birth; bay horses are usually born chestnut with fawn colored markings. 'Grey' horses are born their genetic color and then lighten as they age until they are pure silver white or fleabitten. Also remember that white markings, usually used to identify horses, disappear as the grey horse ages. The colt in the top photo grew into the young stallion under saddle. In a few more years, he'll be the same color as his momma.

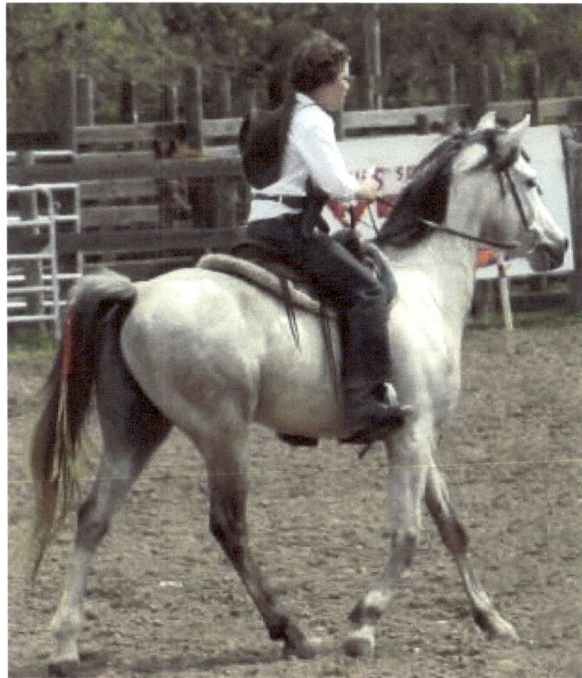

* One of the most common things that always make me roll my eyes and giggle is the shiny black horse. There are some that stay shiny black, but relatively few. Most of them have to be kept inside a barn to keep their color. Sunlight and sweat bleaches the color to a kind of muted orange or an uneven rusty old gold.

* There are incidents of unusual colors or patterns which can be an expression of a rare recessive genetic trait, an anomaly such as the chimera or a spontaneous mutation. I have a filly whose color is not a known genetic possibility, and she's the first one people notice. No one shrugs or looks past it. I've been vehemently accused of misrepresenting her parentage. Some love her, some call her a freak, but they all stare because she's an oddity. Unusual looking horses draw a lot of attention and your characters should have appropriate reactions.

Mistake Three - Terms

Any profession, sport or industry will have its in terms and phrases, all of which are strongly affected by culture, time and place. This can make it especially difficult for the non-horseman to know what's correct, but in many cases, the most important consideration is consistency. In modern day North America, a horse will wear a halter and pop a splint. In Europe, he'll wear a head collar and throw a splint. If he's wearing a cowboy saddle he'll lope, and if he's going English he'll canter. Tack, or tackle, is all the stuff the horse wears: saddle, saddle pad or blanket, and bridle. A bridle is the thing a horse wears on his face when you ride and is a combination of the headstall, bit or bosal, and reins.

I mentor a lot of new riders in my barn and there is always confusion over the seemingly odd contradiction, specificity and overlap of terms. Many of these terms are also used as verbs. "I'm going to tack up the horse," or "go ahead and saddle". The dressage saddle has a girth that holds it on the horse; the western stock saddle uses a cinch. These are different kinds of things that have the same purpose. If a horse has been backed it means it's carried a rider at least a couple of times. When you bridle the horse, you put the bridle on its face. When you bit a horse, it's a training term for teaching the horse to carry a bitted bridle.

* A stallion is not a stud, he "stands at stud". The stud is the farm. Referring to a stallion as a stud is a colloquial use and can be used in dialogue to give flavor to a down to earth or old-school character as opposed to some hoity-toity who's concerned about showing off how correct they can be.

* In modern times, a stallion is an intact male of breeding age, an altered male is called a gelding and a female of breeding age is a mare. A foal is a young horse, the boys are called colts and the girls are fillies. In times past, a stallion was referred to as a horse and a foal was called a colt so the youngsters would be either a horse colt or a filly colt.

Mistake Four - Showing Pain

Authors tend to anthropomorphize horses when they show one in pain but horses simply don't react to pain in the same manner as people.

Aside from walking out to the barn and finding a puddle of blood on the ground, I've learned that knowing a horse is in pain is more a matter of seeing what's not the same than noticing any sign in particular. What's missing from their usual habits or what's different in their manner or attitude? Are they not as curious as usual? Is this the second time you've seen them rolling? The corollary is that it's often just as hard to figure out if something hurts or if they're just saying "don't do that".

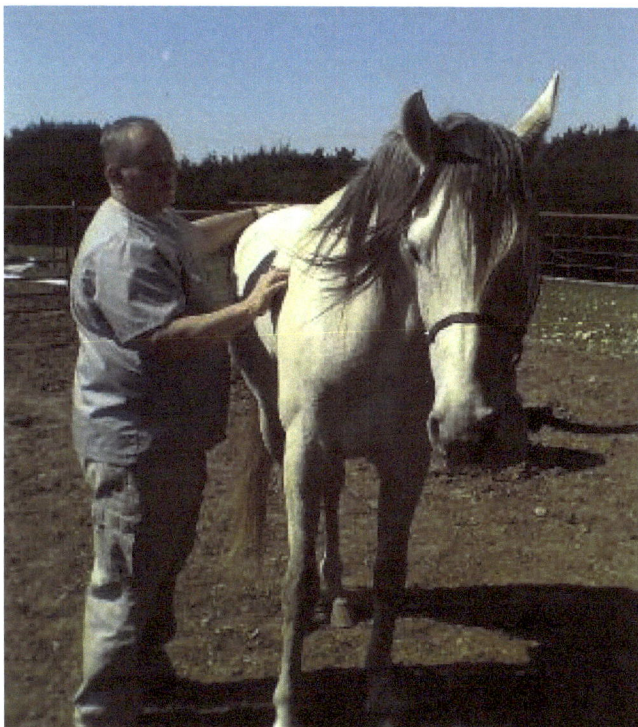

* Horses do not respond to pain verbally. If it's an injury they'll shift the weight off that leg. They typically suffer in a withdrawn way that looks dejected or sullen.

* If you strike a horse, depending on the horse, it will try to get away, even running over you if it has no other choice. Its third option will be to attack in defense of itself.

Mistake Five - Other Equid

Donkeys are too often unfairly characterized as nothing but recalcitrant little beasts without a thought or a reason. They aren't that, but neither are they small furry horses with long ears. Mules are neither donkeys nor horses, but will have characteristics of each.

We have a donkey. He was accidentally weaned too early and so we bottle raised him. Everything I'd ever thought about donkeys, he has redefined. He's highly intelligent and steadfast, his opinion is seldom swayed.

* A donkey does not think like a horse. In many cases he's less reactive and more reasoning.

* A donkey does not act like a horse, he'll tend to look before he leaps. If you try to startle or rush him, you'll more likely only slow him down.

Mistake Six - Travel Times

Authors often seem to misjudge their horses' pace during the heroes' travels. Old cavalry records are available, but they typically record the slowest reasonable pace because they're moving supplies along with the troops, whereas long distance race records reflect the opposite extreme. It's not necessarily true of many modern stall-kept horses, but in the case of historical or fantasy works, the thing to remember is that a fit horse can move at a moderate pace for most of a day. Consider that most horses, such as a working cow horse, can easily do 25 miles a day with a couple of rest breaks. Extreme heat, high winds and difficult terrain such as mountainous trails, mud, deep sands or thick woods can slow them down dramatically. Through AERC competitions, I've ridden 50 miles in 4 hours and I've ridden 100 miles at a time, taking almost the full 24 hours for completion. In order to keep a horse healthy for a long or a fast ride, the rider's focus must stay on the horse. If the rider is euphoric, grumpy, exhausted or injured - the horse will likely suffer for it. Conscientious riders are tuned in to both the horse and the world around them.

* Conscientious riders will allow the horse a period of walk at the beginning and ending of the ride; this allows the horses mechanical and metabolic systems to warm up and cool down more efficiently.

* Fast rides are going to be relatively short. Over any distance, the trot should be the gait of choice in most cases. To ride a long way fast, use intervals of faster and slower gaits. At a walk or jog-trot, a horse can travel indefinitely as long as they're fed and rested several times a day and at night.

* Because of certain specifics of equine physiology, a horse can gallop past the point of having the metabolic resources to live. The often die from complications of exhaustion.

Mistake Seven - Gaits

Please don't have your hero "gallop off at a trot". Gaits are counted by the timing of the hoofs. A walk is a four-beat gait, trot is two beats. A lope or canter is an easy three beats, a gallop or dead run is faster and implies the horse is going about top speed.

Although I have seen people sway and just topple off a standing-still horse, most people are able to ride the walk. It helps if you can figuratively unhinge your back at the base of your spine and roll your hips like a belly dancer, but it's not necessary. The trot requires a sense of balance and timing that most people don't have naturally. I typically start new riders in a pattern that includes only three steps of trot at a time because most people need to rebalance at that point. The canter tends to be an easy-to-ride rocking chair kind of gait that an inexperienced rider can manage if they're bold enough. Sports such as snow skiing and enduro motorcycle racing require the same type of relaxed balance and coordination as riding the horse at a lope or gallop.

* An experienced rider such as a western cowboy or a medieval hero on a quest will be as comfortable on a horse, at any gait, as they are on the ground and it wouldn't be unusual for them to do anything they would routinely do standing or sitting at a table.

* Most horses have three standard gaits. Walk, trot and canter. There are many gaited breeds such as the Tennessee Walking Horse, Peruvian Paso and Standardbred that have additional gaits, meaning different footfall patterns such as the foxtrot, the rack, or the pace. Consider doing deeper research if you use a gaited horse in your story as the terms are breed specific.

Mistake Eight - Falling Off (a)

Everybody falls off. Everybody. Even heroes. The more you ride, the more times you will come off. Now, most probably, as your number of rides increase, the percent of purposefully dismounting in a proper fashion will increase and your unplanned flying dismounts will decrease, but the fact is that someone who rides 1000 or more hours a year has exponentially more potential for disaster than someone who rides 50 hours a year. Someone who spends enough time on a horse to be really comfortable will more likely have issues such as complacency, over-confidence or inattention. Aside from the fact that 'bad stuff happens' they'll be more likely do something stupid and get hurt.

Been there, got the t-shirt, wore holes in it, used it to wash the car, threw it away, and eventually earned another t-shirt. Umm. Stupid… yeah. Sometimes.

* If you can't knock your hero off his horse, at least toss another main character in the mud or over a fence.

* Horses fall down too. Moreso when they're tired or being fractious. If you can't knock someone off, take the horse down.

Kudos to John Ringo, not just for putting his Council Wars hero, Herzer, on a gelding, but for knocking him off and giving him a head injury.

Mistake Nine - Staying On (b)

Of course, the flip side is that too often when a hero does come off, it's with too little effort on the part of the horse. It shouldn't be easy to get them off unless they're being completely inattentive; most average riders can stick three or four jumps before they're bucked off. A competent rider will be accustomed to their regular horse, aware of any usual tricks, and will be on-alert when they're riding an unfamiliar horse. Most competent riders can stay with a skittish horse when they're jigging and dancing around. Perhaps the most difficult transition is going from a large horse to a small one because smaller horses can tend to be quicker than expected and many horses will spin and bolt when they have been startled.

I've been riding young horses and problem horses most of my life and shamelessly use *The Clutching Spider* at need. This is an undignified maneuver in which the rider's arms are thrown about the horse's neck and the back of the knee is hooked over and clamped down on any available protrusion on the saddle.

* A competent rider who is attentive to her horse is not going to fall off if a horse rears or half-heartedly bucks.

* A new or panicked rider can become unbalanced and fall off simply from the motion of the trot or canter. A competent rider will not come off so easily.

Mistake Ten - Diggers and Bucket Bangers

I can't remember ever reading a hero waking up in the middle of the night, cursing and fumbling about for a rock to throw at his horse. Most horses get bored if they're not moving and even after a long day, they wake up in the early morning hours and have nothing to do but wait. Some horses will stand quietly, but others will not. They'll bite and tug on the rope or anything they can reach; some will paw incessantly with a front hoof until they've dug a hole where they're standing. If they play with the rope long enough, they'll untie themselves; whether they hang around camp or leave depends on their relationship with the hero.

We spend a lot of time on the road with our horses, more often camping than not. It seems they get attention deficient in the early morning hours and will routinely fuss until I come out and check on them. My stallion likes to root in his bucket. He'll stick his nose in it and bump it against the trailer until I come out and use harsh language on him.

* If the hero has a fractious or high energy horse, it should cause trouble in the camp. If it gets untied from its tether, it may rummage through the camp supplies. Many horses will dig at boxes or bite bags and shake them out to get at the contents.

* A busy horse will have myriad scars and scraps from picking fights not just with other horses, but with ropes, barns, trees, fences - anything and everything they've tried to get to play with them over the years. This is the horse that can unlatch gates to let everyone out and open doors to get into the grain.

Mistake Eleven - Communication

A horse is often written standing quietly behind the hero as if they don't have a thought or opinion. Nothing could be farther from the truth. Their minds are going all the time and if they know you're listening, they'll let you know what it is they're thinking. They'll tug the reins or nudge their handler. They'll know someone is coming down the road long before anyone comes into sight. They'll let you know if 'something isn't right', with you or them or if there is something in the woods.

One reason I love raising my own foals is because they fall naturally into an open dialogue that promotes the kind of trust that allows for a deeper bond, not just with me, but with any person who will be open to them. Some of the most special moments I've had with other horses are those magical instants when they realize I'm listening to them and asking for a dialogue rather than just making demands.

* Aside from the stallions talking trash to the ladies, most equine communication is non-verbal; a tensing of the eyes and lips, a tilt of the ear, the twitch of a hind leg.

- Horses tend to be very alert and aware of the world around them. They'll almost always alert the handler with ears forward and head raised if someone is approaching.

Mistake Twelve - Gender Bender

Back to stallions. It's well known they've been used as war horses throughout history and are commonly used in day to day activities even in modern times, but so often authors put their characters on horses they call stallions and write them as quiet and docile as geldings. There are more differences between stallions and mares and geldings than just the plumbing. Stallions tend to be high energy with tremendous enthusiasm and motivation. Even a well-trained stallion needs to have his focus managed by his handler. Mares tend to be opinionated and bossy. Mares are natural leaders; stallions are natural followers - as long as you have their attention. Geldings are natural followers who will more easily keep their focus where you point it.

I have ridden and handled stallions most of my adult life, but I was still somewhat unprepared to bring one home. We managed, but the most amazing thing was the noise. They talk - all the time. I was used to the mares' and geldings' occasional nickers and calls, but having a stallion in the yard is like having a looped recording of the boys' locker room bragging about Friday night.

Stallions are noisy. They nicker and huff and whuffle and scream like a wookie. All the time.

Mares would rule the world if they had thumbs. Most of them have a strong natural inclination to be in charge and are quick to question and argue. They don't always go down the trail easily if they're not sure you're right about safety or direction.

Mistake Thirteen - Illness and Injuries

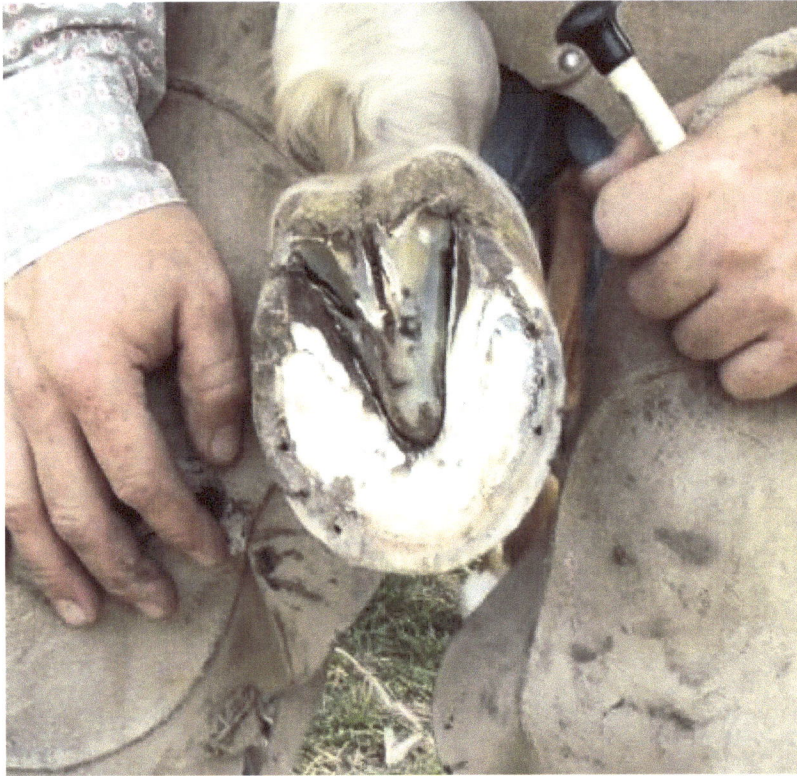

Injuries and illnesses seem to be a difficult area for authors because the obvious injuries are usually the least severe and I frequently read of horses recovering from things they shouldn't or, conversely, having complications where there would be none. A horse can be blowing snot-wads and hacking their lungs up, never missing a meal, and have a complete recovery. The horse that uncharacteristically hangs back from dinner, seems subtly lethargic, is looking at his belly or lying down, may have the potentially life-threatening condition called colic. A horse can recover from horrific surface injuries, gouges and slices, but a virtually invisible bowed tendon can be permanently disabling.

One of our horses had a brown recluse spider bite last summer. It started as a hard spot but in spite of extensive treatment eventually rotted out a horrific gaping oozing hole that covered about a third of the surface area of the horse's neck. It took six months to heal, but there is only a tiny bald spot and a thin line of a scar.

Horses can get a stone wedged in their hoof. But it takes a particular size and shape of rock. Little rocks don't stick and big rocks don't fit. And it's not an injury. You just pop the stone out and go along your merry way. At most, the horse may have a stone bruise, but that's not going to show up immediately. If you need your hero to have to walk home, the horse could bow a tendon. But the horse won't stop because of it. The hero will have to feel a bobble in the gait and check the horse.

Mistake Fourteen – Training

From the earliest days of domestication of the horse through modern times, horsemen have never agreed on appropriate training techniques. Regardless of the technique, someone will take offense because they know what's written is wrong. The important thing for the author to remember is to have the characters use training methods that are both appropriate for their world and for their character.

My personal experience has been that most horses are willing to please if they understand what you're asking and it isn't painful. Some are quite eager to please and with those you sometimes have to be careful what you wish for.

* Horses are prey animals and most of them can be beaten, forced or frightened into doing the handler's will most of the time. These methods tend to work over the short term and with aggressive handlers, but won't establish a bond of trust or companionship with the horse.

* Horses are absolutely hierarchal and if you're too sweet, soft, gentle and kind, they take that to mean that you're being submissive and are asking them to take care of you. There is a middle ground of firm leadership that works well with most horses.

Mistake Fifteen - Drinking & Exercise

It's a common misconception that an exercising horse shouldn't drink water. Up until the studies done prior to the 1996 Olympic Summer Games in Atlanta it was widely believed that hot horses should have their intake of cold water restricted and that they shouldn't have cold water poured on their bodies. Authors should carefully evaluate their characters' background to know how they would water the horse.

When I jumped into riding AERC Endurance in the late '80s, I landed in a good crowd of experienced long distance horsemen. Endurance has grown and changed in many dramatic ways over the years, but the importance of letting horses drink as much as they want is an overarching part of a newbie's education in the sport. Not only do the vets emphasize that point, but courtesy (supported by peer pressure) demand that riders, as a group, water together on the trail. The horses' continued health is of primary concern to endurance riders and this is shown by even the most competitive riders when they'll stop and wait for a competitor to water their horse.

* An exercising horse must have water.

* While, factually, a horse can and should drink as much as he needs (although he needs to keep moving after) people have habitually let the horse have only sips at a time until it was completely cooled out.

Mistake Sixteen - Mares in Labor

Mares might get peevish, but they don't scream, whimper, cry or whinny in pain and fear as they go through labor.

We bought a mare we didn't know was pregnant. Not having breeding dates, we didn't have a due date. She started showing signs of labor in October and didn't deliver until the end of January. Sleep deprived doesn't begin to describe my condition by the time she foaled. But that's typical of mares. They'll never do what you expect, when you expect it. People like to fret, fuss, prepare and watch and watch and watch and - the minute you drift off to sleep or sneak a potty break, you come back and find a foal. Without a doubt they do that on purpose.

* For all the accurate details of proper foaling, including the things that can go horribly wrong, pick up a copy of Blessed are the Broodmares by M. Phyllis Lose, VMD. But the main thing to remember is that mares won't read the book, so anything they're supposed to do, they likely won't.

* Typically, mares will switch their tails up and down, their butt will get squishy and they'll pace. They may get up and lie down, up and down. Most foals are born easily and quickly.

Mistake Seventeen – Weapons

Because a warrior is trained in the use of an axe, bow or lance does not mean he can jump on any available horse and charge into battle. Horses have to be specifically trained to accept the use of weapons from their back.

I accidentally hit my horse in the butt with the butt of my lance. Once. She thought she'd been attacked from behind. It was not pretty.

* Using weapons from the ground and on horseback are similar yet different skills because the rider's seated position changes both the balance and angle at which the user wields the weapon.

* A horse unaccustomed to the swinging, shifting weight of a sword, the thrust of a lance or the bark of a gun is likely to suck back, duck, spin and bolt away from the action instead of into it.

Mistake Eighteen - Breeds and Specific Types

Horse characters often seem vaguely interchangeable rather than showing the specific body types, mentality and training that real-world horses have. While it's expected that a well-rounded horse should be able to fulfill many roles, there will be tasks that come naturally to each horse and others that require more training and effort to accomplish. Some horses are natural jumpers, some love the open road and some are content to go 'round the arena or up and down the field.

The horses in my breeding program are similar in mind and body, but there are still differences between them and I make an effort to find them jobs they enjoy. In return, it seems, they try harder to please me when I ask them to do something difficult or unusual.

* A conformationally balanced, strongly-built, athletic horse should be able to do well at a variety of tasks. The more specialized they are in breeding or training, the higher level of performance they'll have at that one job at the cost of versatility.

There is no such animal as a perfect horse. Let your horse have faults, a long back, a heavy head or a crooked knee and show his heart and the strength of his spirit in doing his job in spite of what ails him.

Mistake Nineteen – Consistency

I'm often reading along and the otherwise quiet, non-descript horse will do something. But horses are creatures of habit. A quiet horse will tend to be steady in everything he does. A skittish horse will be as silly about eating as he is about going down the trail. A lead mare will question and debate endlessly over the speed and direction of the trail and the quality of your characters' companions.

In many ways, consistency, on both the parts of the horse and rider, are the basis of a relationship, be it good or bad. I know my young stallion can be brought out of the pasture, saddled and ridden and his training and generous heart will compel him to try - he'll try oh so hard - to be good. But unless he's been ridden and exercised on a regular basis, that good only lasts about half an hour and at that point his enthusiasm for the trail can get out of hand. Knowing that about him, I'm not surprised when he starts acting silly. I simply keep him focused on listening to me, knowing he'll work through it and we can go on about our day.

* If a horse has done something and received the same response about three times, it will become a habitual. Anything from nipping when the girth is tightened to traveling the same byways, some won't walk past posts where a fence has been.

A fussy nervous horse will not to eat if it's not at home, if the weather is bad, if there are strange horses in the barn, if there are noises in the night or if the feed or water smells different. If you want to give your hero a nervous breakdown, put his war horse out to stud and force him onto a finicky replacement

Mistake Twenty – Memory

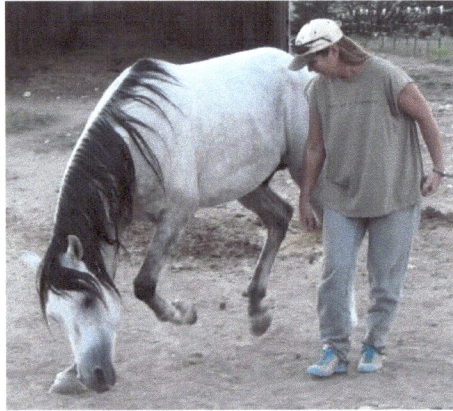

Everyone knows about the elephants' memory, but aside from 'Ol Faithful bringing the drunk groomsman home each night, no one seems to mention it in regards to horses. They have wonderful memories that are a tremendous boon in training but can be a hindrance in re-training horses that have been misused. They remember a kind word as well as a raised hand, although it pays to remember that their trust may be hard-earned.

I've found, as much as I love working with them, a highly intelligent horse can be more difficult to train not only because they can be creative but because they tend to pick up on unintentional cues. My young stallion is trick trained and he's extremely sensitive to my body language and mood. There have been times when he's done something I didn't intend, but when I laughed it was reward enough that he started repeating the behavior. It's a problem because some things are cute once but quickly become obnoxious.

* Horses will remember a trail once traveled, even over a number of years, and they almost always know the direction home.

* Behaviors (such as standing still while a rider mounts an ill-fitting saddle) that are rewarded with pain won't be repeated; those rewarded with kindness or treats (such as nudging open the feedroom door to find a barrel of grain) will be.

Mistake Twenty-One – Anthropomorphization

Modern authors seem to pride themselves on differentiating horses from other types of livestock. They are both right and wrong. Horses do think and feel emotion, but not human thoughts or human emotion.

One of the most interesting things I have learned about the equine thought process is that they don't define a difference between "taking care of" and "being the boss of". It's only one concept to them. The lead mare says when and where to drink. The herd melts out of her path when she walks through and follows her when she walks away. And she's the first line of defense against the wolves. People seem to have a difficult time understanding that if they insist the horse mind its manners, then the horse will find comfort and confidence in knowing the person will take care of, feed and protect them.

* Horses are not "just dumb animals". They do think and have opinions and emotion.

* Horses are large prey animals - their first line of defense is flight. They do not have a human thought process or human motivations.

Mistake Twenty-Two – Pedigrees

So many times the hero grabs the first horse that comes to hand, but that shouldn't be the case unless he has no choice. Most horsemen are attached to their horses and are more wound up about their horses' ancestors than the stodgiest Hobbit ever dreamed of being. The typical horseman knows less about his grandmother than he knows about the looks and habits of his favorite mount's ancestors as far as they can be traced. The antitheses being the few who vehemently deny the concept of genetics and insist that crooked legs and bad temperament are all a matter of luck.

Through the years of line-breeding, I've seen the quality of the ancestral breeding stock come through clearly. I have several sub-sets of horses that are closely related through repeated grand parents - they resemble each other and their ancestors more than their immediate sire or dam. I've seen that while the foal's natural temperament is inherited from both the stallion and the mare, most of the foal's attitudes and habits are taught by the dam.

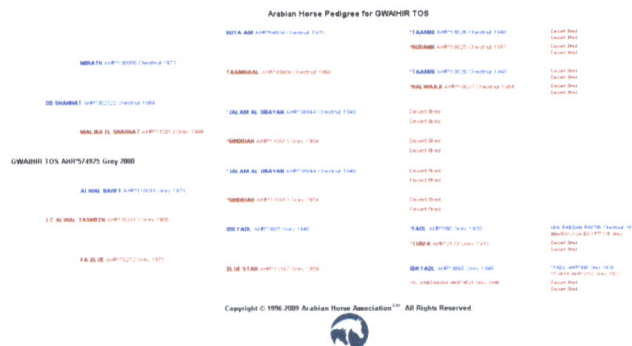

Arabian Horse Pedigree for GWAIHIR TOS

* Genetic traits are not aligned toward the Light or Darkness; they simply exist. If a horse's pedigree has more crooked legs than fewer, it's likely to produce crooked legged foals. If a horse's history is filled with brave, stout-hearted mares, it's likely to produce brave, stout-hearted foals.

* There will always be exceptions

Kudos to Holly Lisle in Talyn for Talyn's dilemma over the bay Tand mare's pedigree, acknowledgement of the responsibility of replacing quality stock and overall conscientious breeding practices.

Mistake Twenty-Three - Signs

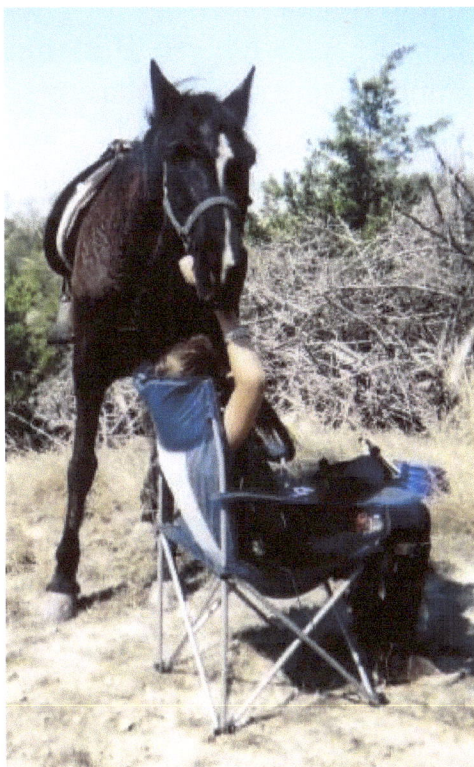

Checking on the horse in the corral seems to be analogous to checking the warmth of a car's hood to see if it's been running recently, but it's not the same. Unless the horse is still blowing and dripping sweat, it's hard to tell how long he's been standing. A better measure would be to check for fresh fecal balls, or lack of. Since horses tend to poop on a regular basis, if they've been in the corral more than a couple of hours, there should be some fresh piles, unless it's a very active horse. High-energy or excitable horses will scatter the balls into dust with their pacing.

Horses are all about subtle signs, but they tend to be highly individual - you only know something's wrong by catching what's not-normal for that horse. It's hard to tell if a horse has a sore back or ouchy legs unless you know that horse's individual response to palpation of those areas. Ears sticking out sideways instead of front or back can mean they have ticks or a burr lodged inside or it could only mean they are highly perturbed. Purple lipstick spots mean they've been eating prickly pear fruit.

* Sweat marks matted in the hair do not show how long it's been since a horse has been ridden. They can stay in for weeks if a horse is winter-wooley. They only show the horse wasn't groomed after its last ride.

* Saddle marks, white patches of hair on the horses' back, have been touted as proof that a horse is well broke. They do mean, to some extent, that a horse has been ridden a lot of hours - with a saddle that fit so unevenly that the pressure points killed sections of the horse's skin, causing the hair grows in white.

Mistake Twenty-Four - Fantasy Horses

If it looks like a horse and people of that world use it to ride or drive or plow; it should be something like a horse. If it's not a horse, make it not a horse. If it's more like a horse than not, instead of giving some new thing horse-traits, try starting with a horse and adapting some traits to better fit the environment and culture of that world. In a dysoptia, far future, or other-world consider the environments that shaped real world horses before mounting characters on your current favorite real-world breed. Best examples would be the differences between desert Arabia with its tough little Bedouin horses or the draft and carriage breeds of medieval Europe. There are magical instants, in this mundane world, when one will look me in the eye and I hear the whisper, "believe", and I do.

* Horse's lips are prehensile, more like a short trunk than long lips. They physically can't form the kinds of sounds we use to speak out loud.

* Selective breeding over the long term will eventually reproduce the desired characteristics, be it speed, strength or beauty. Working horses are in all things functional; pet projects tend toward one extreme, defaulting to dysfunctionality in other traits. With few exceptions, these traits (both good and bad) should be reflected in the general equine populations of the people of your world.

Kudos to JRR Tolkien for capturing the nobility in the hearts of horses with his wonderful Mearas. From the fantastic Nahar of old to the indomitable Rochallor, who died of grief after the loss of Fingolfin, to Shadowfax, not only for his unflagging speed crisscrossing Middle-earth, but for being steadfast in enduring the terror of the Lord of the Nazgul.

Mistake Twenty-Five - Harness Horses

Other than basic horsemanship, very little about riding applies to harness horses. One interesting difference is that while riders are typically hurt when they fall off the horse, drivers are not normally injured by falling out of the wagon, but by being run over by it.

The first time I got in a cart and went for a drive was amazing. It was exhilarating in ways I hadn't expected and, I'll admit, a little frightening. I found it very disconcerting to be so in-contact and yet, at the same time, so distant from the horse.

* All the stuff that goes on the horse is called harness, not tack. The horse is harnessed and put to the cart, not hitched to the cart. Afterward, he's unhitched and unharnessed.

* Any style of two-wheeled vehicle is called a cart. Carriages, wagons and buggies have four wheels.

* Driving and riding are two different skill sets. Many horses are trained for both, but not all.

Mistake Twenty-Six - War-mares

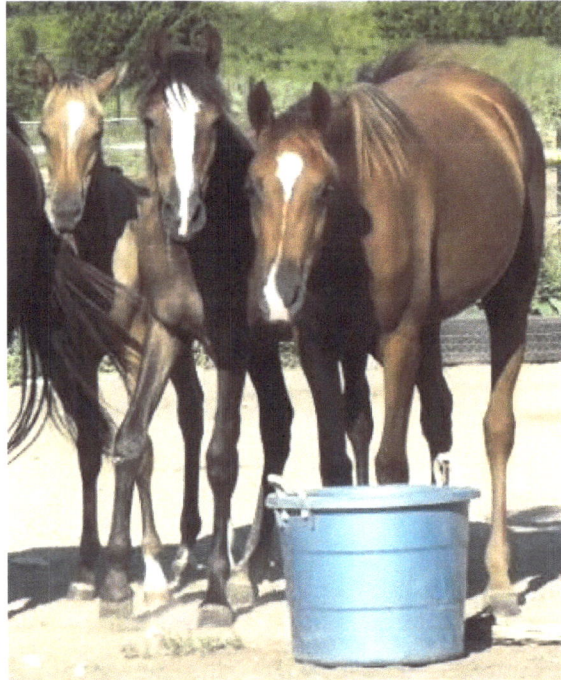

In our real-world history, the Prophet Mohammad and his followers conquered the known world from the backs of their tough little desertbred mares. These mares were so precious to them that the stewardship of the purebred horses became wrapped up as part of their religion.

My experience with war mares came in a 'round about way. As I acquired my herd of Bedouin-bred Arabians, I started learning how little I really knew about horses. My first lead mare is now a grand old lady although she was young and full of herself when we met. The day she arrived was the start of a cold war that lasted for years, until she taught me that I could step back and trust her to do her job - keeping the herd safe and orderly. Her colts are raised to "yes ma'am" and "no ma'am" and are happy for it. Her daughters are raised with the training they need to rule the world, should they have the opportunity. They are strong, confident girls, deceptively quiet as long as everything is in its place. I have a young mare now, MIREE, who is coming into her own and demanding to take her place beside me as a partner. It's humbling to see her aggressive protection of me and I can well see trusting her to defend my life.

* A warhorse that's a stallion can be more like a berserker that you have to aim and loose in the direction of the enemy.

* Not only will a war mare fight intelligently, but she'll work with your balance to stay under you and is likely to carry you to safety if you're injured.

Kudos to Patricia Briggs in Hob's Bargain, not only for the big hearted workhorse, Ducky, and Kith's yellow gelding, Torch, but especially for the Lass, Wendel's delightfully peevish war-mare.

Mistake Twenty-Seven – Names

Horses are too seldom named in novels and it just doesn't ring true. There is something personal and special about a horse and even the gruffest old men tend to name their horses. There are some common naming conventions: western characters tend to name their horse by its color or marking, such as Blaze, Red, Buck or Socks. Farmer's horses have simple names ending in -y such as Missy, Daisy, Lady, Billy or Fugly. Little girls names their horses after their heroes and fantasy horse names should have at least three syllables.

It's common to name horses after fictional characters and, with stars in my idealistic young eyes, I combed the index of JRR Tolkien's The Return of the King to compile a list of names for all the horses I would someday have. Over thirty years later, Peter Jackson's movies exploded the stories' popularity. I switched to naming my foals in Quenya rather than using existing names on my list, but I already had my Wind Lord. When I loose the reins and let him fly I'm reminded that dreams do come true.

* Horses, at least personal horses that characters spend time with, should have names.

* The names must be culturally consistent.

Mistake Twenty-Eight - Ages

Many authors seem to somehow equate horse years to dog years and that leads to myriad inaccuracies. Horses mature at a slower rate and the modern horses' lifespan is well over 20 years with many living well into their 30s. Much of that is due to better health care although their lives can be dramatically shortened by extended periods of abuse such as malnourishment and over-use, especially during their youth.

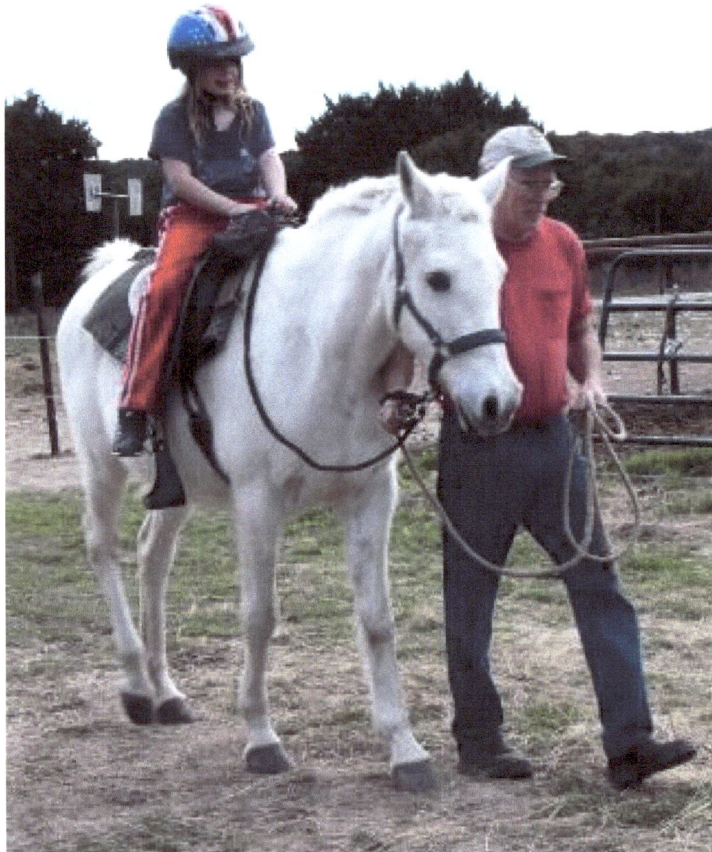

There is a unique and special beauty to every age of a horse, from the soft tickly nose and sweet breath of a curious foal to the quiet steadfast calm of an oldster. More and more, it seems to me, there is a special quality, so often overlooked, in the proverbial old grey mare. She tends to be the safe one, the smart one, the one you can trust to take the kids over the mountains and bring them home again. Because she's been there and done that. She knows where the water holes are and how to get through the secret passage. And she tends to have an inner strength that keeps her going in spite of old legs and a swayed back.

* Young horses have been overworked in the same way children have been throughout history into modern times.

* While it's accurate to portray characters using horses as young as 18-20 months old, a horses' skeletal system isn't completely mature until they are fully eight years old. Overwork stresses and molds the still growing skeletal system and strains the soft tissues of the support system.

Deb Bennett (online) has exhaustive research showing details and information on progressive breakdown due to overwork of young and unprepared horses.

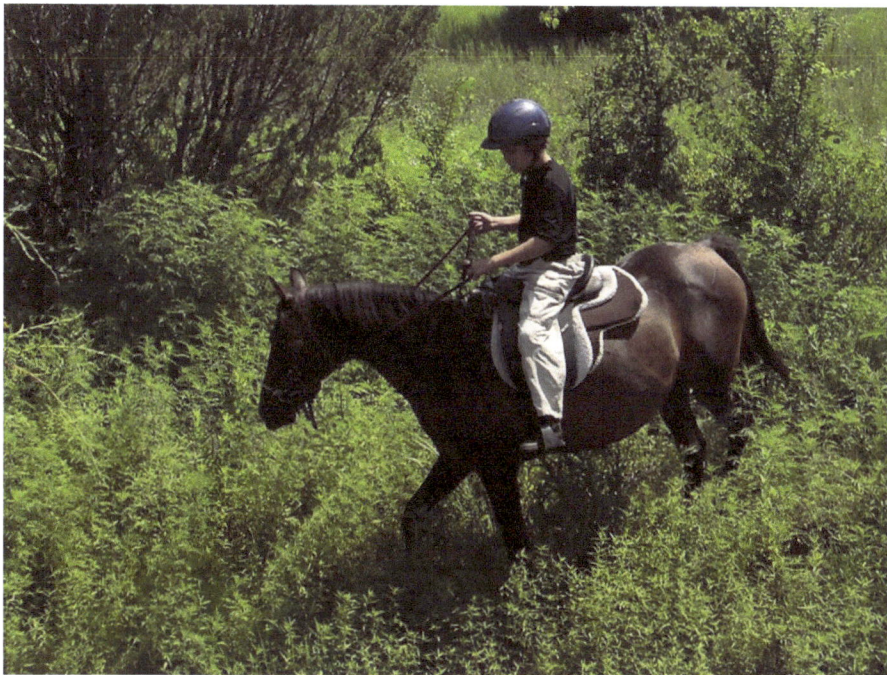

Mistake Twenty-Nine – Feed

I'm not one that cares to read every detail and every step of the way but book after book without even a nod to the horse being fed makes me wonder how they don't all starve to death and leave fantasy-land depleted of mounts. At least I'd like to know that the hero lets his horse graze each night of the quest rather than just tying him to a tree in the dark.

As many years as I've had horses, I've run the gamut from measuring micro-amounts to just making sure they have hay. I've come to realize why feeding programs work, or don't, is based on day to day consistency. If they get most of the stuff they need, most of the time, they do pretty well with it. I am adamant about them having plenty of forage and an overall high quality of feed, but I don't sweat the daily grind. I do have horses here who suffered extreme neglect and malnutrition in their youth and while they've had happy productive lives, they never had a chance to reach their potentials.

* Horses can subsist on an amazing variety of food stuffs, from prairie grass, oats, corn or even dried dates, but for growing foals and performance horses to reach their potential, they should be fed correctly according to their specific needs at the time. They need to graze on a regular basis. Studies have shown that they'll start forming ulcers at about four hours past their last meal.

* Horsemen are an odd lot about feeding. Some will fret and measure and weigh every feeding, others just toss a scoop of grain in the bucket. Still others don't feed grain, only giving the horse access to native pasture. But without fail, devotees of each system are adamant that what they're doing is right and everyone else is silly or abusive.

Mistake Thirty - Daily Care & Inanities

Other than the common rubbing down, and the proverbial bucket of oats, we seldom see a hero taking care of his horses and this is a missed opportunity for characterization - to show how he treats a beast when no one is watching. It's said that characterization is defined by putting your character under stress and showing his reaction. What about 1000 pounds stepping on his toes? I understand that lords and ladies have stableboys to cool down the horse, groom and muck out the stalls, but characters on the trail, or those with less amenities, should show some care for their horses.

You shouldn't chew gum while you poop-scoop a stall, especially bubble gum. If you do, chew with your lips shut or, at least, don't blow a bubble. You don't want to know how I know, but a hint would be that the dust in the air flavors the gum unfavorably.

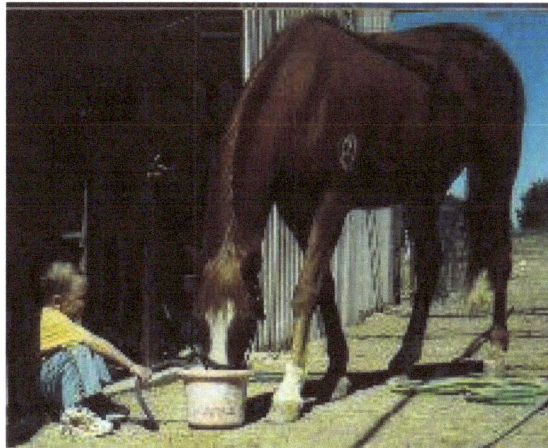

* Horses require a certain amount of grazing and water. If they are working they need grain, whatever is native to the area. If they are traveling they need time to graze during the midday break and at night.

* Horses require a great deal of grooming. Working horses require daily grooming to keep the coat clean so accumulated sweat and dirt doesn't cause saddle sores. If an unused horse is brought up for use, he'll likely have tangles in his mane, his hoofs may be too long and his coat muddy and rough.

Mistake Thirty-One - Does Size Matter?

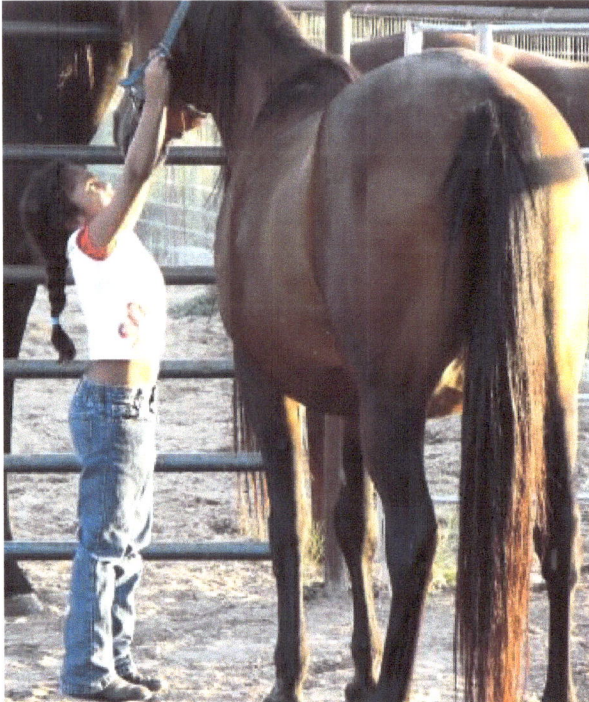

It's almost always unclear to me what size horse the hero is riding, as though horses only came in one average size. Or maybe big or little, but those are comparative phrases and depend on the horse being bigger or smaller than some unidentified average. Horses' heights are measured in hands (hh="hands high"). A hand is four inches and is measured from the ground up to the wither - the high point on the back where the last hairs of the mane grow.

In our American world where bigger is better, I've always been a defender of small horses, under 15hh. I bought WITNESS and her sister by video and knew she was small, only 13.3hh. What I didn't know was how deeply I would fall in love with her. I bought her for the kids and didn't know if I'd be able to ride her. I was, and found her to be as strong and forward as many larger horses. She taught me that while height is part of the equation you must consider how the whole horse is put together, as well as the size of their heart and the strength of their spirit.

* Manly men seem to need to ride big horses, but, within reason, that's more of an emotional tweak than physicality. Factors that determine a horse's size include the width and shortness of their backs and other aspects of their conformation, such as correctly aligned joints and good density of bone in their legs.

* Bigger horses tend to have a higher incidence of lameness over long distance. (Susan Garlinghouse, Tevis95-06)

Mistake Thirty-Two - Injuries to People

Bit, kicked, stepped on, pushed down, bucked off - no one doubts horses can be dangerous animals because of their size. But fictional injuries almost always seem to be minor and I wonder if authors are unaware of a horse's strength.

Although I do believe there are real outlaws, I refuse to debate if they are born mean or made that way through mishandling. Most horses won't purposefully hurt people and most injuries come from people startling horses, getting in the way of a frightened horse, getting between two fighting horses, or getting tossed off for whatever reason. If a horse has in his mind that he's going to hurt somebody, chances are he will cause a serious injury at some point. I've seen a mare bite a two year old gelding in the neck, pick him up and toss him about ten feet. A person doesn't have any chance against a horse that's intent on doing damage.

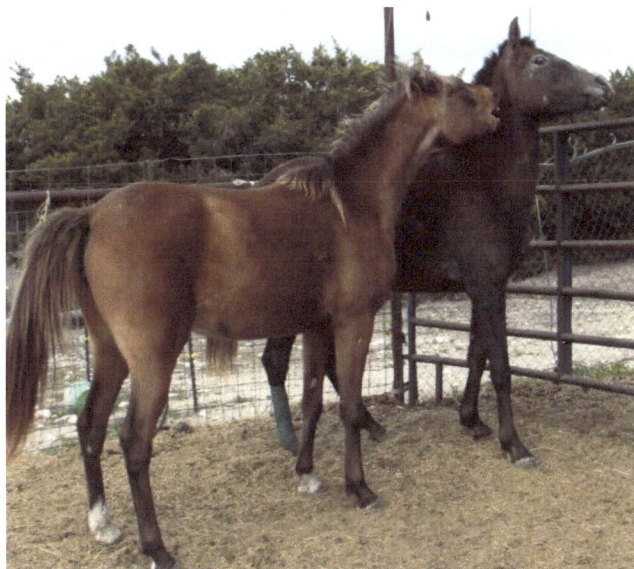

* A horse can easily kill a person either with a direct strike or kick, or by complications arising from either. A horse is strong enough to break bone with its bite. They can easily pick a person up and toss them ten or fifteen feet.

* It's not unusual for mares to severely injure and even kill people who try to handle their foals.

Mistake Thirty-Three - Don't Try This At Home

Because they can do stupid stunts in the movies doesn't mean readers will buy your hero succeeding or even surviving if they pull those same stunts. If it's actually been done in real life, remember that exceptions happen and unless you have the supporting framework of extenuating circumstances and resulting consequences, your readers are unlikely to maintain their suspension of disbelief.

Some times I feel like Moe Bandy and Joe Stampley should sing a country western song about my life. It can be funny, if you're the kind of person who likes to drink too much, to brag about being kicked out of bars or locked up for a couple of nights in the slammer, but those wild hairs stretch a little thin as we age.

Certainly I know the old adage that truth is stranger than fiction. I've survived things I feel would be difficult to justify in a story, such as driving my truck off a vertical drop that just happened to be exactly as long as the wheel-base of my long-bed 4-door Chevy pickup so the horse trailer stopped perfectly safe and level instead of being pulled over. I've been bucked off a young horse and landed on my face; I've turned horses over sideways and flipped them backwards off a bank; I've been stuck inside a horse trailer with a panicking horse and I've been trampled under water - twice. There's no excuse for that kind of thing except for sheer youthful stupidity. So when I read these types of things, having seen them from the other side, I have less belief rather than more because I know I shouldn't still be here. I know my guardian angels are battered and worn from keeping up with me and that characters wouldn't really be able to survive many of those movie tricks without authorial intervention.

* A horse, especially a heavily muscled stock horse, can not run endless miles across the desert without feed and water.

* An untrained feedlot rescue can not go on to win a Prelim Event in a matter of months, even with professional training.

* If you gallop to the edge of a cliff and flip off the horse's back and hold onto the reins, the horse's head and neck might be able to support you, but the bridle would not.

* Because you've made friends with a horse on a desert island by feeding him does not mean you'll survive that first ride.

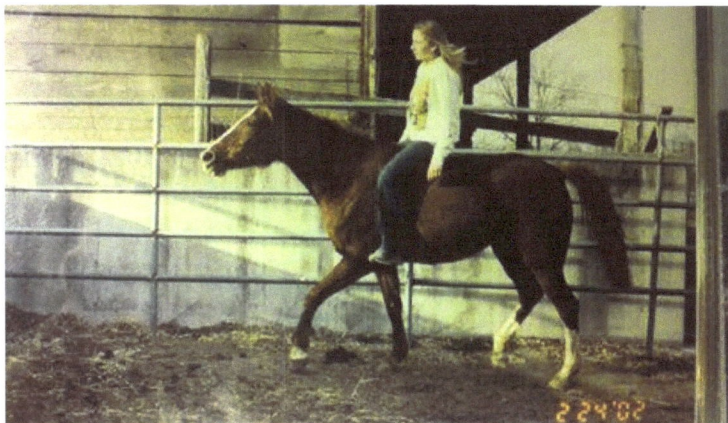

* Because a horse had a minimum of training in his youth does not mean he's going to be manageable 15 years later. Especially if he's an outlaw stallion.

* Tackless riding is a highly advanced test of training, trust and riding ability. Highly advanced. Horse and rider as a team.

* Galloping across anywhere you can't see the ground. Amber waves of grain, and more especially their wild native cousins, are likely to have uneven ground, holes and other unpleasant surprises hidden at their roots.

* A complete fracture of the cannon bone will not heal with herbs and stall rest.

* It's inhumane to jump off the roof of a building onto a horse.

* Galloping downhill at speed - not a good idea. Galloping down a steep hill in a heavily wooded area - a really not good idea.

Conclusion

Here are some resources I recommend to help you increase your knowledge and write believable horses.

* BLUESue writing and riding - horses in our daily lives, how habits and incidents can be used to add conflict, humor and depth to your stories with equine characters.
http://bluesuel.blogspot.com/

* Fantasy Horse Stable - A virtual stable of horses with photos and details on each horse.
http://fantasyhorse.blogspot.com/

* http://www.DonnaSnyderSmith.com/- clear, comprehensive detail on how to do it right - horses, how to handle them, riding and training effectively with specifics in many sports and disciplines.

Recommended additional reading:
Anything by Linda Tellington Jones, Tom Dorrance or Gawani Pony Boy
Conditioning Sport Horses by Hillary M. Clayton
Horsewatching by Desmond Morris
Dressage in Lightness by Sylvia Loch

With all this in mind, authors who write horses should notice horses in other author's books. A few favorite authors who write horses effectively:
Holly Lisle: especially Talyn and Rose Sea
Patricia Briggs: Hob's Bargain
Carl Raswan's Drinkers of the Wind
L'Amour: Not just his westerns, but also in Walking Drum.
JRR Tolkien: great love & respect for them with minimal characterization

Many many THANKS to A Conspiracy of Authors

What is the conspiracy? They are a group of authors conspiring to bring readers excellent material by making their work accessible to as many people as possible. They feature fiction and nonfiction and both short and long publications, mostly in electronic format, but with print books as part of our future.

Look for the rest of the 33 Worst Mistakes books, they are available in a wide variety of topics at http://www.aconspiracyofauthors.com/ or most online bookstores.

I sincerely appreciate your purchase of this course and hope you find it interesting and helpful. If you need more detail on any topic, please don't hesitate to email me at BLUESue22@gmail.com or visit my blog at www.WritingHorses.com or my website at www.BeckyBurkheart.com

Please remember to recommend me to your writer friends and to review online to help other authors choose this valuable resource.

As a final note, all the horses pictured are purebred Arabian horses, but more than that, they belong to a breeding group known as BLUE STARs. Many of these horses are as close as second or third generation from actual Bedouin war-mares that were ridden in raids in the Nejd as late as the 1960s. Legend records the Bedouin horse being selectively bred for over two thousand years as a war-horse and a companion to man. Those that couldn't tolerate the harsh desert conditions, the raids and battle, or who weren't companionable with their people, didn't survive to reproduce.

The breeders of these extraordinary horses greatly value those qualities and strive to maintain and reproduce the duality of fierce boldness and confidence combined with a true nobility and gentle spirit, and a compelling desire to bond with an individual rider. The owners of these horses are proud to share them here simply because they love sharing the enjoyment of their horses.

More information about this unique group of horses can be found online at www.BlueArabianHorseCatalog.org or search facebook for our page and group.

happy horses, happy trails,
Becky Burkheart

www.ingramcontent.com/pod-product-compliance
Lightning Source LLC
Chambersburg PA
CBHW060833270326
41933CB00002B/69